Lockheed Constellation 1945

Lufthansa
Boeing 737 1968

TWA
Boeing 707 1958

PAN AM
Boeing 747-100 1970

Douglas DC-3 1936

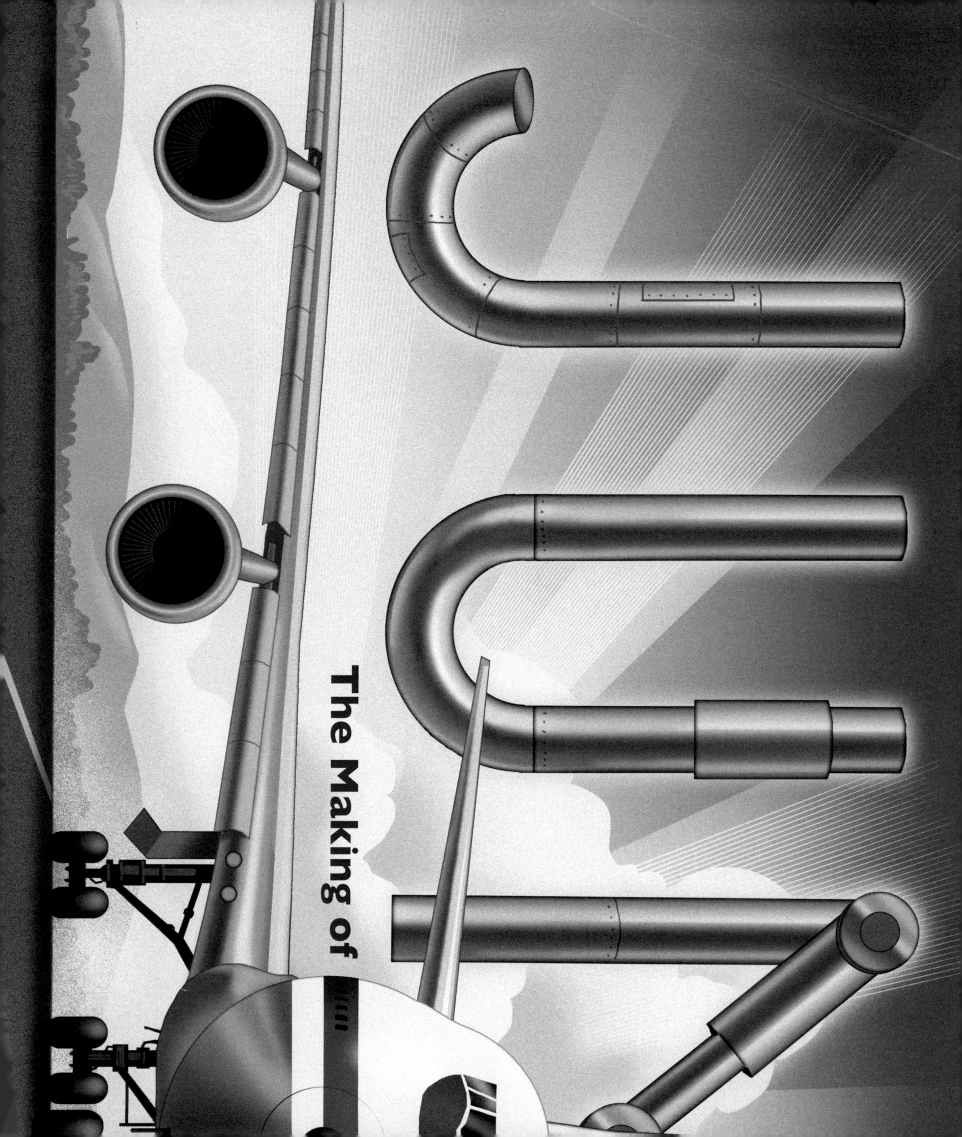

The Making of

the Boeing 747

CHRIS GALL

ROARING BROOK PRESS
NEW YORK

People say the Queen of the Skies can for
moments be seen in a rainbow's light.

—Li Bai, Chinese poet, 701–762 CE

On September 30, 1968, the biggest passenger jet the world had ever seen was rolled out of the assembly plant. Thousands of people had come from around the world to watch. Cameras flashed and people cheered. The giant plane was made by the Boeing Company and called the Boeing 747, but reporters named it the "jumbo jet."

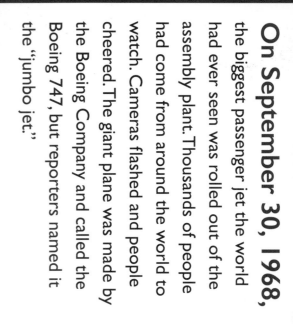

There was only one problem.
The plane couldn't fly.

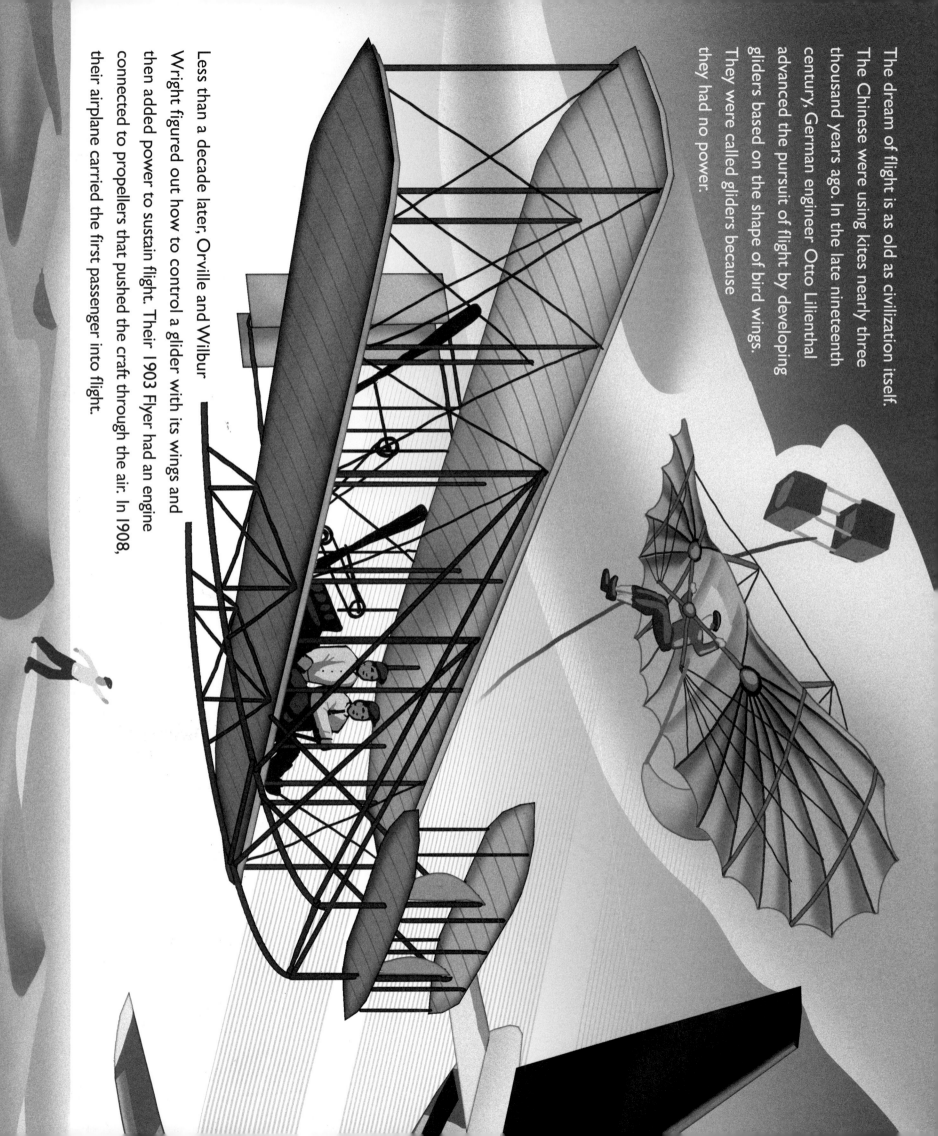

The dream of flight is as old as civilization itself. The Chinese were using kites nearly three thousand years ago. In the late nineteenth century, German engineer Otto Lilienthal advanced the pursuit of flight by developing gliders based on the shape of bird wings. They were called gliders because they had no power.

Less than a decade later, Orville and Wilbur Wright figured out how to control a glider with its wings and then added power to sustain flight. Their 1903 Flyer had an engine connected to propellers that pushed the craft through the air. In 1908, their airplane carried the first passenger into flight.

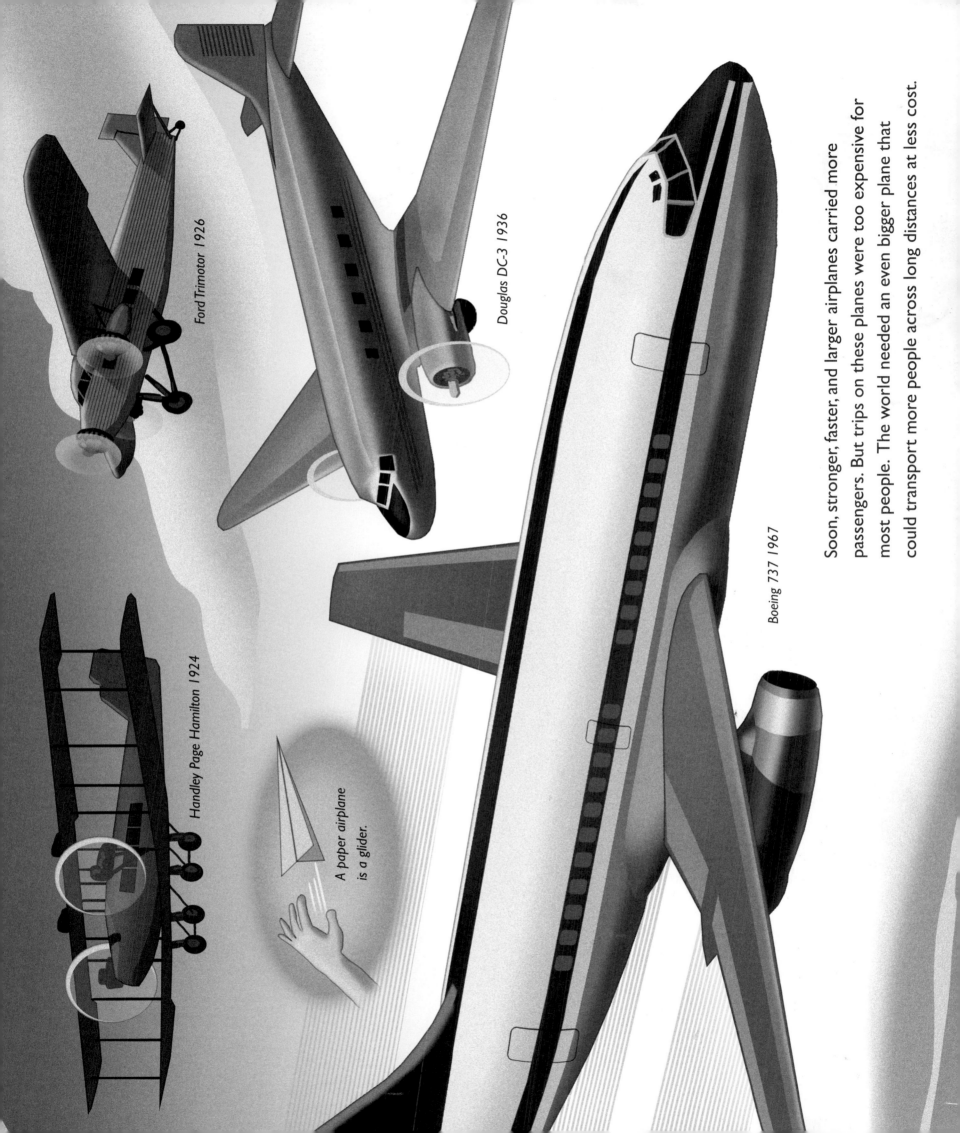

Ford Trimotor 1926

Douglas DC-3 1936

Handley Page Hamilton 1924

A paper airplane is a glider.

Boeing 737 1967

Soon, stronger, faster, and larger airplanes carried more passengers. But trips on these planes were too expensive for most people. The world needed an even bigger plane that could transport more people across long distances at less cost.

The president of Pan American World Airways dreamed of such a plane and asked Boeing to design one. It would be two and a half times larger than any other passenger jet at the time. But how could such a big plane fly?

Four important forces are at work when an airplane flies: **gravity, lift, drag,** and **thrust.**

These forces were the same for the Wright brothers' first plane and for the Boeing 747 jumbo jet. Engineers would have to figure out how to overcome gravity and drag with lift and thrust.

Drag

Gravity

Lift

Thrust

Lift is the force that works against gravity to keep a moving object in the air. Airplanes' wings give them lift. Air passes over the wings faster than it passes below, creating a difference in air pressure that causes the wings to rise.

Air flow

Lift

Wing

Gravity is always pulling objects down. The heavier the object, the more gravity pulls. There is a lot of gravitational pull on a plane as big as the Boeing 747.

Gravity causes your ball to drop.

The Boeing 747 would need huge wings. The bigger the wing, the more it can lift. But speed also affects lift, and planes move more slowly on takeoff and landing. Then the wings need even more lifting ability, because the airflow over the wing is slower.

The main body of a plane is called the **fuselage.**

Leading edge flaps

Wing ribs

Fuel tank

Airplane wings have movable flaps that make the wing wider to increase lift. The pilot controls them from the cockpit, retracting them when the plane reaches a certain speed after takeoff and extending them as the plane slows for landing.

Flaps

Airflow

Drag

Thrust

Thrust is the force that works against drag to keep objects moving forward. For airplanes, engines provide the power to create thrust, which pushes the wings through the air and causes lift.

Drag slows objects as they move through the air. All moving objects, including airplanes, have some drag. But the smoother the shape of a plane, the less drag.

Holding your arm out a car window while moving causes drag.

The earliest airplane engines used pistons and gasoline to turn a propeller, which creates a difference in air pressure that propels the plane. Propeller engines grew larger and larger as planes grew bigger and bigger, but they could only create a certain amount of thrust.

Propeller

Pistons

In-line piston engine

Pistons

Propeller

Radial piston engine

Larger planes needed even more power. They needed jet engines. The first jet engine was a turbojet. It sucks in air, compresses it, and mixes it with fuel, then ignites the mixture. The flaming gas passes through a turbine and shoots out of a nozzle at the back of the engine, pushing the plane forward. Turbojets use a lot of fuel and are very loud, but they move planes much faster through the air.

Turbine

Air

Turbojet engine

Exhaust gases

The Boeing 747 was no ordinary jet plane—it was a jumbo jet—and it would need even more powerful engines to get off the ground.

When you run, your legs provide thrust.

Before the Boeing 747 could be built, it had to be designed—but what would it look like? Some thought it should be like a double-decker bus. But while that design could carry many people, it could not be evacuated quickly. Engineers decided a wide, single deck would be best.

They did, however, move the cockpit to a small second level on the top of the plane so the nose could be lifted open on freighter models to load cargo. This gave the plane a distinctive hump. The hump would be the plane's most recognizable feature.

To try out their design ideas, engineers made models and tested them in a wind tunnel, a special chamber with a gigantic fan pushing air through it. Engineers could measure how different shapes and angles for the wings and body affected airflow, lift, and drag, and see how a full-size plane might fly at different speeds.

The new plane would be so big that Boeing's factories were too small to manufacture it. So the company built a factory in Everett, Washington. Trees had to be removed, land excavated, and a railway constructed to bring in sections of the plane. It would be the largest building in the world by volume, and remains so to this day.

Pan Am was eager to get the first jumbo jet in the air and gave Boeing only twenty-eight months to deliver the 747. That was just over two years to bring into service an aircraft that only existed on paper. Boeing started construction of the plane even before the factory was finished—there was no time to waste!

The plane was built in sections. Many sections were built by other companies in different parts of the country and had to be shipped to the new factory in Everett by rail and truck. All the pieces had to go together perfectly—there are over 4.5 million pieces in a 747! Half of them are fasteners, like rivets, screws, and bolts.

Model airplanes are also made in sections.

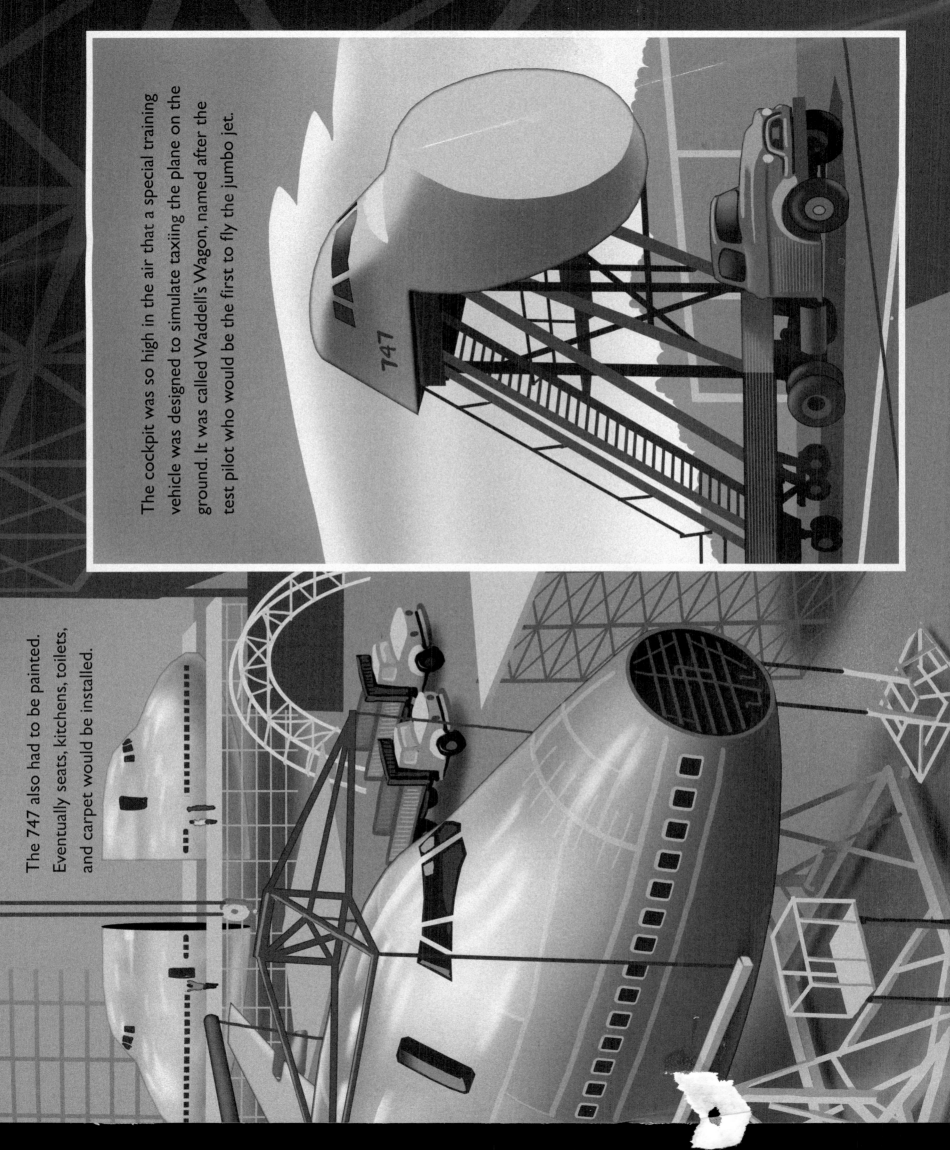

The cockpit was so high in the air that a special training vehicle was designed to simulate taxiing the plane on the ground. It was called Waddell's Wagon, named after the test pilot who would be the first to fly the jumbo jet.

The 747 also had to be painted. Eventually seats, kitchens, toilets, and carpet would be installed.

747

Since the Boeing 747 was so huge, the new landing gear had to be huge, too. The jumbo jet would need eighteen wheels instead of the standard ten to distribute all that weight.

Large pistons move the landing gear up and down, and special doors open to stow the gear inside the plane. With the wheels tucked away, the plane's shape is smoother, reducing drag.

The 747 was the first two-aisle passenger jet. This feature became known as a "wide body." The broad design could hold as many as 490 people. It even had a lounge upstairs in the hump, where first-class passengers could relax.

Economy class seats

Menu

747

Meals on the 747 were prepared in galleys and served on plates. The seats were comfortable and had lots of legroom. The 747 was the first jet to have closable overhead bins for passengers' belongings.

Cockpit

Staircase

Lounge

First class seats

Baggage compartments

A plane must be designed to be as safe as possible. Damage to one important piece could spell disaster. Normally, each important system has a built-in backup plan in case of failure. This is called redundancy. In the case of the 747, each important system had multiple backup measures in place for even more safety.

Life raft

Oxygen mask

Planes carry oxygen masks in case oxygen levels drop inside the cabin, as well as life preservers and rafts in case of a water landing.

Life preservers will keep you floating in water.

In an emergency, planes have to be evacuated quickly, within ninety seconds, per federal rules. This was accomplished with extra—and wider—doors and inflatable slides. Local residents were used to test final evacuation procedures. The people were individually numbered so that engineers would know exactly where they had been sitting in the plane.

The cockpit is the most important place in a plane. All controls, levers, and gauges are collected there so the pilots can fly the plane and the flight engineer can make sure all systems are working properly.

Pilot

Flight gauges

Rudder pedals

Throttles

Yoke

CHECKLIST 747

Copilot

Aircraft systems control panel

Flight engineer

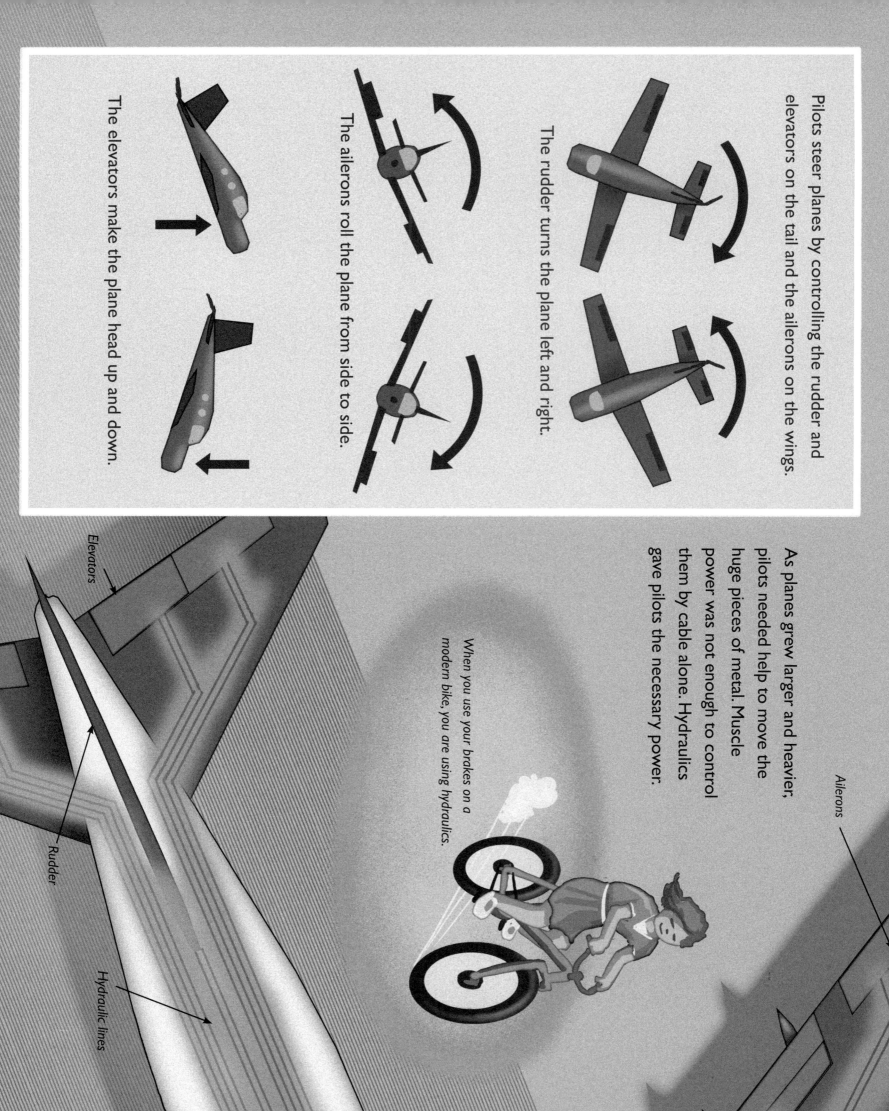

Pilots steer planes by controlling the rudder and elevators on the tail and the ailerons on the wings.

The rudder turns the plane left and right.

The ailerons roll the plane from side to side.

The elevators make the plane head up and down.

As planes grew larger and heavier, pilots needed help to move the huge pieces of metal. Muscle power was not enough to control them by cable alone. Hydraulics gave pilots the necessary power.

When you use your brakes on a modern bike, you are using hydraulics.

Elevators

Rudder

Hydraulic lines

Ailerons

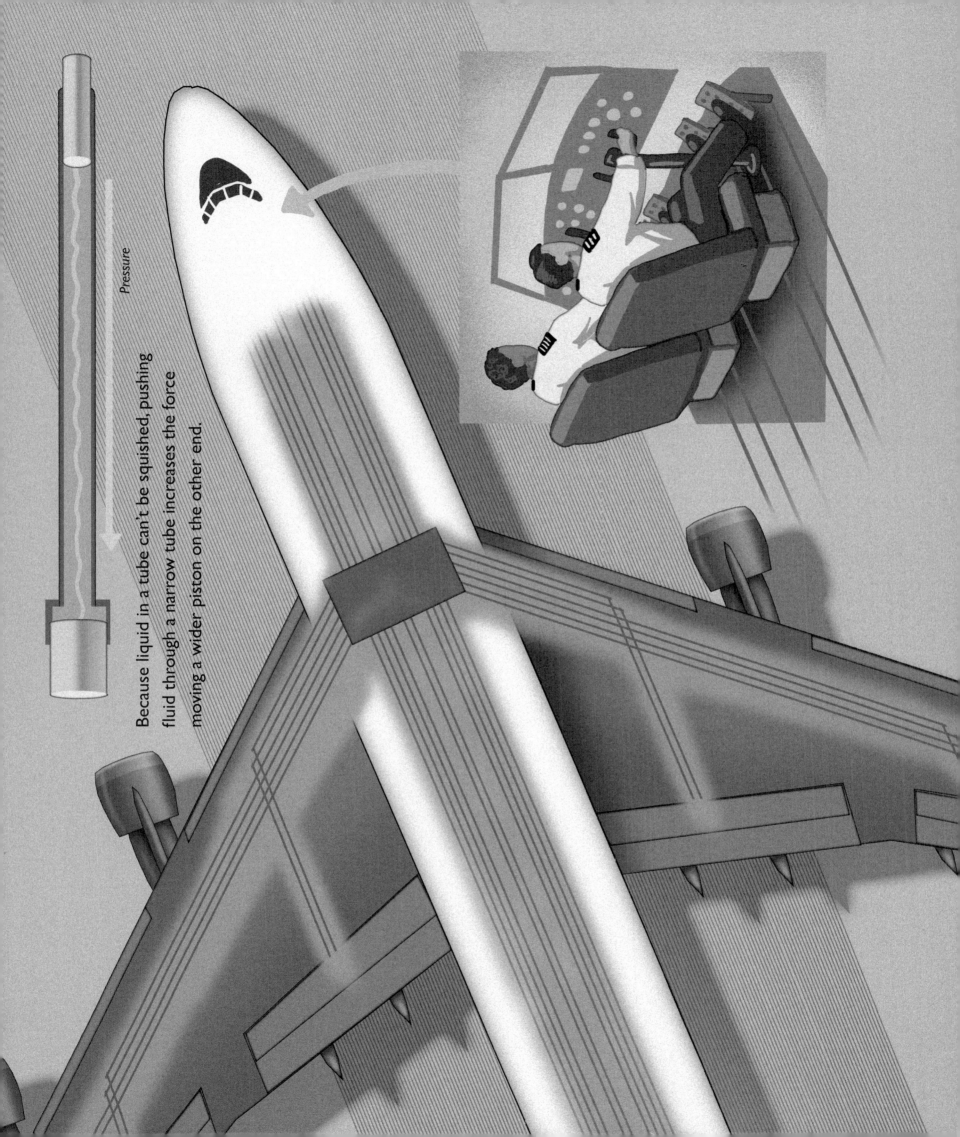

Pressure

Because liquid in a tube can't be squished, pushing fluid through a narrow tube increases the force moving a wider piston on the other end.

Finally, after twenty-eight months, and with the help of thousands of people, the mighty plane was ready to be shown to the public. But it was not ready to fly. When it rolled out of the assembly plant to the cheers of an excited crowd, the engines under the wings were only for show.

The real engines were still being developed and tested, and many parts had yet to be installed. The engineers were racing against time to meet the deadline.

The Boeing 747 was so big that it needed the latest engine technology to power it, a high-bypass turbofan. It was bigger than a turbojet and gulped much more air, which gave it more thrust and made it quieter.

A few months later, it was finally time to see whether the largest passenger jet the world had ever seen could fly. It would take the skills of three brave men—two pilots and a flight engineer—to take it into the air. Employees gathered and held their breath. Would it fly?

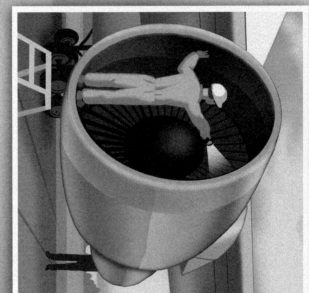

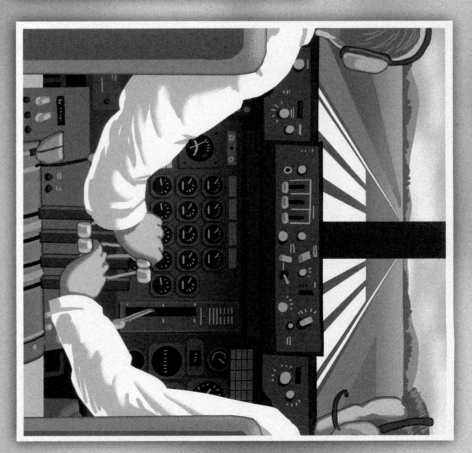

After all flight checks had been performed, it was time to find out. A small chase plane would accompany the 747 to observe how it flew. The runway was clear. All engines were running. The plane was cleared for takeoff!

The pilot pushed the throttle forward to full power, and with a huge roar, the giant plane began to move forward.

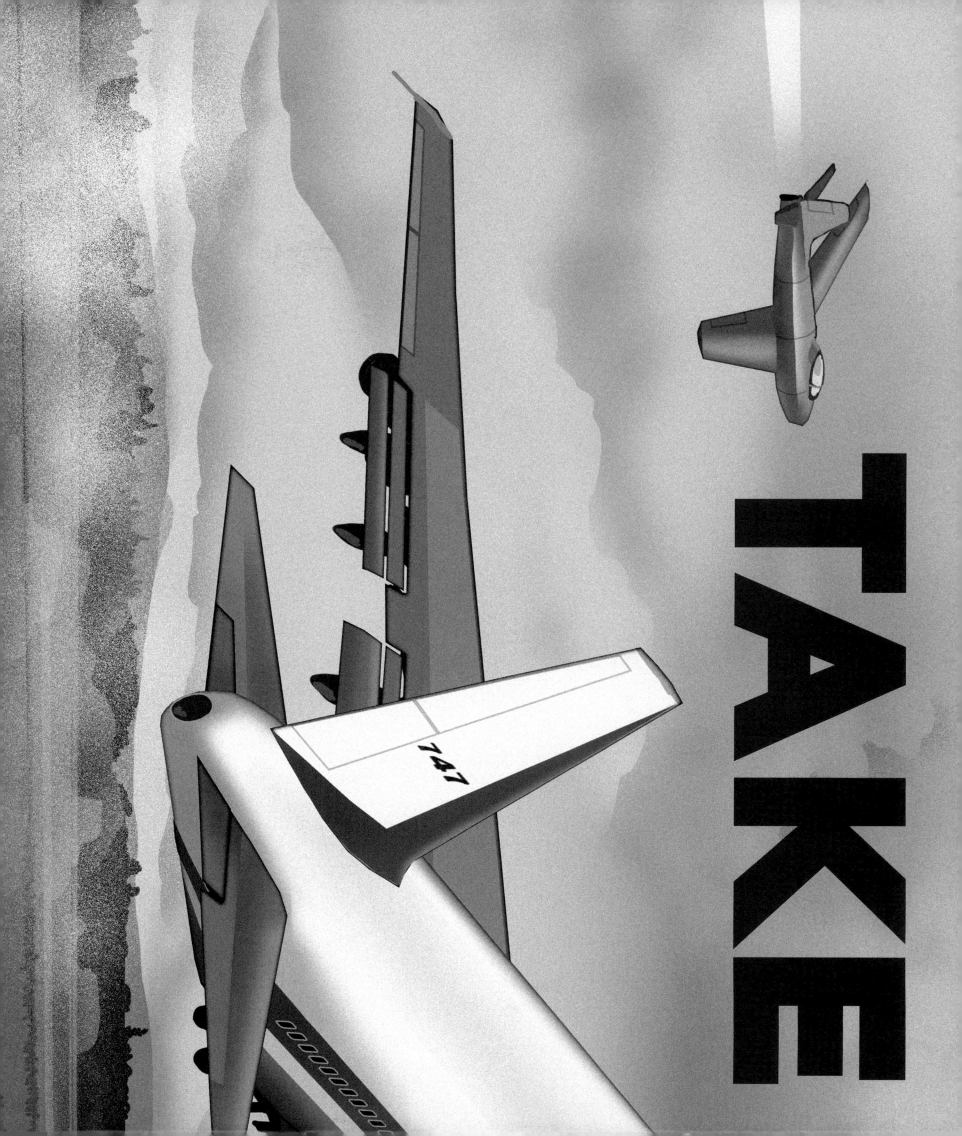

All new planes must be tested before they are declared safe to carry passengers. For the 747, five planes were used to test different aspects of the jumbo jet's performance. Each carried cameras and specialized equipment to record data.

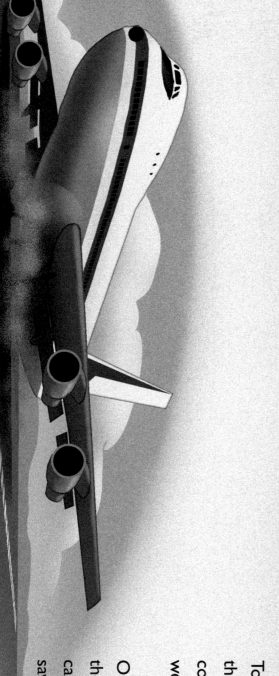

To see how the plane handled different loads, more than 175 water barrels were installed. Engineers could pump water between barrels to shift the weight during flight.

One test plane was damaged on landing, tearing off the right wing's landing gear and damaging its engine casings. The plane and eleven people onboard were saved due to the 747's redundant safety measures.

The first commercial flight of a 747 was on January 22, 1970. It was a Pan Am flight from New York to London. Excited passengers were amazed at the size and space inside the cabin.

The plane was so quiet, many passengers could not hear the engines, and few felt the wheels touch down a little more than six hours later in London. The world had never seen such a beautiful plane. And because of its size, many more people could now discover the world at a lower cost.

Forty-eight years later, in 2018, the last jumbo jet to fly passengers for an American airline flew off over the horizon. Newer, lighter, and more efficient aircraft had replaced the 747. But for millions of people who have flown in one, the 747 will always be …

the Queen of the Skies.

FUN FACTS

In 1984, Lynn Rippelmeyer became the first woman to captain the Boeing 747.

NASA used a modified 747 to ferry the space shuttle from landing sites back to the Kennedy Space Center in Florida.

The men and women who designed and built the jumbo jet were nicknamed the Incredibles because of their hard work. Ten million labor hours went into the plane before the first flight.

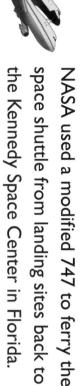

The Global 747 SuperTanker is the largest firefighting aircraft in the world. It can hold nearly twenty thousand gallons of firefighting chemicals.

The Boeing 747 has transported the equivalent of 78 percent of the world's population.

Nearly half the world's air freight travels by 747.

When airplanes reach the end of their lives, some are recycled, some are scrapped, and some are put to creative use. One 747 is now a hotel, with two rooms in the engine casings. Another became a restaurant. The wings of one 747 make a roof for a house in Malibu, California.

The assembly building in Everett, Washington, was so big that clouds would form up in the ceiling rafters.

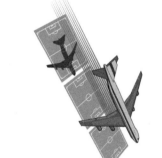

The first jumbo jet was 231 feet long and 196 feet wide, and the tail was as tall as a six-story building.

The latest 747 can travel the length of three soccer fields in one second. It still is the fastest commercial passenger plane in the world.

The Wright brothers could have flown their entire first flight inside the fuselage of a 747—and still stayed inside the economy section.

GLOSSARY

aileron—Movable surface on the wings that banks the airplane for turns

cockpit—Compartment at front of a plane where pilots control flight

drag—Force that opposes motion of an object through air

elevator—Movable surface on the rear of the plane that pitches the plane up and down

flap—Movable surface on the wings that creates more lift

fuselage—Main body of an airplane

gravity—Universal force between all matter that draws objects together

hydraulics—Use of contained liquids to move objects

lift—Upward-acting force that works against gravity

piston—Moving part of an engine that creates power

propeller—Device that consists of a central hub with spinning blades that create thrust

redundancy—Built-in backup systems for the purpose of safety

rudder—Movable surface on the tail that turns an airplane left and right

taxi—To operate an airplane on the ground under its own power

throttle—Lever that controls the power of an engine

thrust—Force that drives an object forward

turbofan—Jet engine in which a turbine-driven fan provides additional thrust

turbojet—Jet engine that expels hot gases to produce thrust

yoke—Steering wheel a pilot uses to control the ailerons and elevators

SOURCES

Boeing Company. boeing.com.

Irving, Clive. *Wide-Body: The Triumph of the 747*. New York: William Morrow, 1993.

Spencer, Christopher, dir. *747: The Jumbo Revolution*. Documentary. Smithsonian Channel, 2013, smithsonianchannel.com/shows/747-the-jumbo -revolution/0/3407070.

Sutter, Joe. *747: Creating the World's First Jumbo Jet and Other Adventures from a Life in Aviation*. New York: HarperCollins, 2006.

Wood, Chris. *Boeing 747: 1970 Onwards (All Marks)*; *Owner's Workshop Manual*. Minneapolis: Zenith Press, 2012.

AUTHOR'S NOTE

It is not a simple, or easy, decision to build an airplane. But in 2007 I decided to build one of my own. Like Boeing years before, I had to calculate cost, the time involved, and where I would find the space to build. I spent six months doing careful research before I decided which type of plane I would build. I measured my garage carefully. I had just enough space to assemble the plane—even though the wings would have to be removed in order to get it out when I was finished!

Finally, after months more of waiting, the fuselage frame and a hundred boxes of parts and raw materials were delivered to my house. Even though the plane was called a "kit," it had very few manufactured parts. Ninety percent of the plane would be manufactured by myself alone. I would need to learn dozens of new skills to accomplish this feat. Drilling, riveting, fabric covering, painting, wiring, and electrical design would all be accomplished through research and, often, trial and error.

Three years later, the Kitfox was ready to be transported to the airport, where it would undergo final assembly and first flight. It took eight strong family members, a large flatbed truck, and nerves of steel to get it there. Three months later, after the engine had been tested, the moment was at hand. On my birthday in November 2010, I decided to get all my hard work into the air and see what this airplane could do.

No first flight of any new airplane goes perfectly, and mine was no exception. So when the engine overheated and sprayed coolant all over the windshield, I was ready and did not panic. First I flew the Kitfox carefully back to the airport and landed softly, with a great sigh of relief. First flight accomplished! And just like the 747, the Kitfox had many hours of testing ahead before it could carry a passenger.

My trusty Kitfox is still flying to this day, and I can recall no greater sense of accomplishment every time the wheels leave the earth.

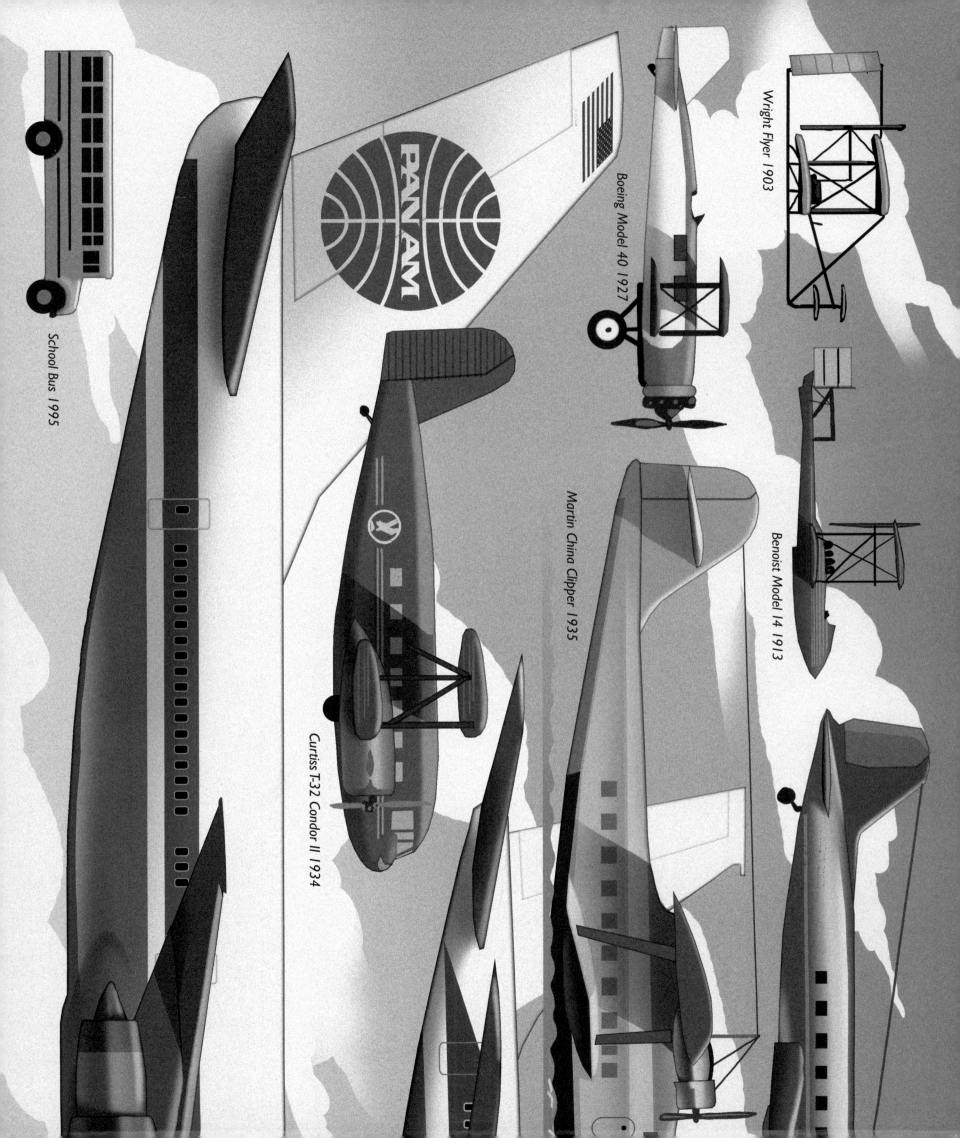

School Bus 1995

Curtiss T-32 Condor II 1934

Martin China Clipper 1935

Boeing Model 40 1927

Wright Flyer 1903

Benoist Model 14 1913